Works for String Orchestra

Edward Elgar

DOVER PUBLICATIONS, INC.
Mineola, New York

Bibliographical Note

This Dover edition, first published in 2000, is a new compilation of four works originally published separately. Breitkopf & Härtel, Leipzig, originally published *Serenade, Op. 20,* in 1893, and *Sospiri, Op. 70,* in 1914. Novello and Co. Ltd., London, originally published *Introduction and Allegro, Op. 47,* in 1905, and *Elegy, Op. 58,* in 1910.

The annotated contents list as well as the notes on pp. 24 and 32 are newly added. These notes were drawn from *The New Grove Dictionary of Music and Musicians* (Macmillan Publishers Limited 1980), and from information generously offered by the Yale University Music Library.

For their contributions of rare scores, we are indebted to the Sibley Music Library, Eastman School of Music, and to The Edwin A. Fleisher Music Collection, The Free Library of Philadelphia.

International Standard Book Number: 0-486-41388-8

Manufactured in the United States of America
Dover Publications, Inc., 31 East 2nd Street, Mineola, N.Y. 11501

CONTENTS

SERENADE
for String Orchestra
Op. 20
(1892)

SERENADE
for String Orchestra
Op. 20

I

II

III

ELEGY
for Strings
Op. 58

(1909)

ELEGY
for Strings
Op. 58

Mordiford Bridge, 1909.

SOSPIRI
Adagio for String Orchestra
with harp (or piano) and harmonium (or organ) ad libitum

Op. 70

(1914)

Elgar's Violin Concerto, Op. 61, is dedicated to Fritz Kreisler, who gave its first performance, in London, 10 November 1910. The man closely involved in the solo technicalities of its composition, however, was violinist William Henry Reed, a member of the London Symphony Orchestra and its leader for 23 years (1912–35). Reed's friendship with Elgar grew out of their close contact at orchestral festivals as well as through Reed's participation in premieres of Elgar's Violin Sonata, String Quartet and Piano Quintet (Opp. 82, 83 and 84) in 1918 and 1919. Reed wrote two books on Elgar. The first includes sketches for the composer's unfinished third symphony with Reed's commentary on them, based on first-hand discussions with Elgar.

It was to Reed that Elgar dedicated his *Sospiri* ("sighs" or, more loosely, "laments").

Cordially dedicated to W. H. Reed

SOSPIRI
Adagio for String Orchestra
with harp (or piano) and harmonium (or organ) ad libitum

Op. 70

INTRODUCTION
and ALLEGRO

for String Quartet and String Orchestra

Op. 47

(1904–5)

Elgar's dedication of his *Introduction and Allegro* "to S. S. Sanford" reflected the composer's plan to visit America, both to accept a Yale doctorate in 1905 and to conduct his music in that country in 1906, 1907 and 1911.

A formidable but extraordinarily discreet influence on the musical affairs of Yale University from 1894 until his death in 1910, Samuel Simons Sanford was instrumental in introducing music into the Yale curriculum. Independently wealthy, and considered by his peers to be one of the greatest (and least recognized) pianists of his era, Sanford served the university as Professor of Applied Music, sharing the departmental chair for a time with Horatio Parker.

It was Sanford's offer to Elgar of an honorary degree from Yale, in June 1905, that formed the central event of the composer's first visit to America that summer. "You must let him [Sanford] do all he wishes to do," wrote Elgar to a friend, adding that ". . . I have finished the string thing [the *Introduction and Allegro*] and it's all right"—concluding his letter with the postscript:

"I dedicate the string thing to Sanford, bless him!"

To S. S. Sanford

INTRODUCTION and ALLEGRO
for String Quartet and String Orchestra
Op. 47

33

END OF EDITION